JC21.9

YO-DWM-913

Man is the only animal who makes tools and machines. Did you ever stop to think that all the machines you use and see and read about could be broken down into just a few types? These are *simple machines:* the lever, the wheel and axle, the pulley, and the inclined plane. Complicated machines such as typewriters, dishwashers, airplanes, or drill presses are made up of many simple machines.

This book explains simple machines and how they work and then goes on to tell about transmission, waterwheels and windmills, steam engines, tools that make tools, electric power, mass production, and automation.

The "Reason Why" Books

MACHINES

Irving and Ruth Adler

The John Day Company   New York

The "Reason Why" Books
by Irving and Ruth Adler

© 1964 by Irving and Ruth Adler

All rights reserved. This book, or parts thereof, must not be repro-
duced in any form without permission. Published by The John Day
Company, Inc., 62 West 45th Street, New York, N.Y. 10036, and
simultaneously in Canada by Longmans Canada Limited, Toronto.

Library of Congress Catalogue Card Number: 64-20709

MANUFACTURED IN THE UNITED STATES OF AMERICA

Contents

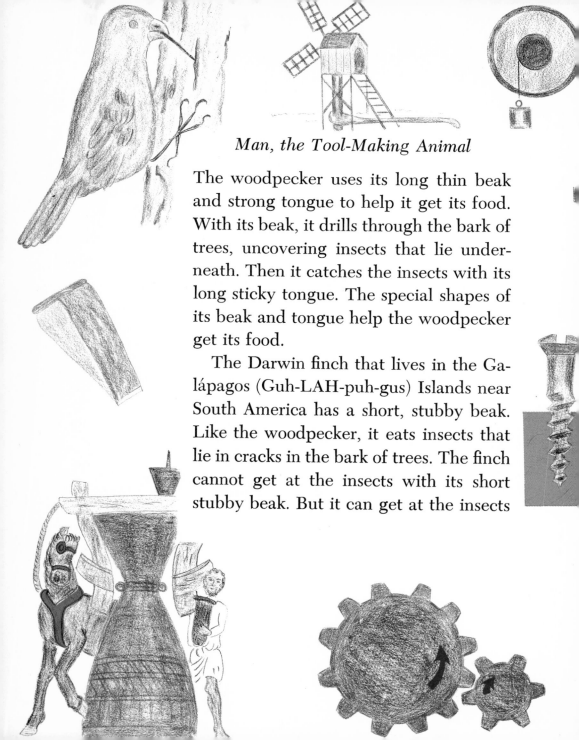

Man, the Tool-Making Animal

The woodpecker uses its long thin beak and strong tongue to help it get its food. With its beak, it drills through the bark of trees, uncovering insects that lie underneath. Then it catches the insects with its long sticky tongue. The special shapes of its beak and tongue help the woodpecker get its food.

The Darwin finch that lives in the Galápagos (Guh-LAH-puh-gus) Islands near South America has a short, stubby beak. Like the woodpecker, it eats insects that lie in cracks in the bark of trees. The finch cannot get at the insects with its short stubby beak. But it can get at the insects

with the help of a small twig or a cactus spine. The finch grasps the spine or twig firmly in its beak and pokes the insects out. When the finch uses a spine or twig in this way it is using a *tool*. It is using a tool to give its beak more power.

The tools the finch uses for getting its food are tools that it has *found*. Man uses tools, too, to help him get his food. The tools that man uses, however, are usually tools that he has *made*.

Man is the only tool-making animal. With the help of the tools he has made, man has learned how to do many things that he could not do with his body alone. With the help of the tools he has made, man is learning to master the world.

What Is a Machine?

Moving men often use ramps for loading heavy objects into their vans. It is easier to load a piano into a van by pushing it up a ramp than by lifting it straight up.

In order to lift a piano straight up, a *force* at least equal to the weight of the piano must be used. This force points straight up. In order to push the piano up a ramp, a smaller force is used. This smaller force points along the ramp's slope.

Using the ramp changes the direction and changes the strength of the force needed to load the piano into the van. A ramp is one example of a tool called a *simple machine. Every simple machine either changes the direction of the force used or changes the strength of the forced used or does both.*

A crowbar is another simple machine. When a crowbar is used to lift a heavy rock, a small force pushing down on the crowbar is changed to a large force pushing up on the rock.

A seesaw is a simple machine, too. A light person whose weight pushes down on one end of a seesaw can raise a heavy person on the other side.

A pair of metal-cutting shears changes the force at the handles to a larger force at the blades. Dressmakers' shears change the force at the handles to a smaller one at the blades. Shears and their relatives, tongs and pliers, are also simple machines.

When we think of machines, we usually don't think of seesaws, crowbars, ramps or shears. We think of things like washing machines, typewriters, airplanes or drill presses. These complicated machines are made up of many simple machines. Because of this fact, the first part of this book will describe different kinds of simple machines and what they do.

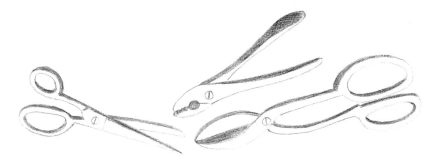

Energy, Work and Mechanical Advantage

There is *energy* stored in the muscles of all living things. The *energy* stored in muscles is used when the muscles do *work*. The energy stored in the muscles of the moving men is used when they do the work of moving the piano up the ramp. In moving the piano up the ramp, some of this stored energy is changed into energy of motion. Some of this stored energy is changed into energy of heat, too, when the piano wheels roll over the ramp. When the piano is resting on the van, the energy of motion has been changed back into stored energy.

Stored energy, energy of heat and energy of motion are all different forms of energy. Although energy changes from one form to another, the amount of energy never changes. Energy is never lost.

The energy stored in the muscles of the moving men...

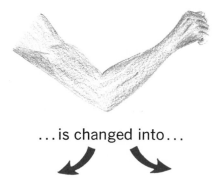

...is changed into...

...energy of motion and energy of heat.

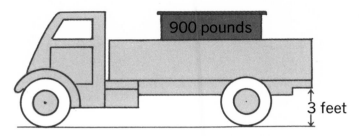

Stored energy is (900 pounds x 3 feet) or 2700 foot-pounds.

Now we can find out why it is easier for the moving men to push the piano up the ramp than to lift it straight up. Suppose the piano weighs 900 pounds. When the piano is lifted straight up, a certain amount of work is done. Suppose the floor of the van is 3 feet above the ground. If the piano is lifted straight up, a force of at least 900 pounds must keep acting through this distance of 3 feet. The amount of work done is found by multiplying the force by the distance through which it acts. So the piano movers do (900 pounds × 3 feet) or 2700 *foot-pounds* of work. When the piano is resting on the van it has 2700 foot-pounds of stored energy in it as a result of having been raised above the ground.

The amount of stored energy in the piano depends only on the weight of the piano and its distance above the ground. It has nothing to do with the way in which the piano was placed on the van. So, if we overlook the energy that is changed into heat, the moving men must also do 2700 foot-pounds of work when they use a ramp to raise the piano onto the van.

Suppose they use a ramp that is 9 feet long. Then the force needed to push the piano up it acts through this distance of 9 feet. What force acting through a distance of 9 feet will do 2700 foot-pounds of work? The force needed is 300 pounds, because a force of 300 pounds acting through 9 feet does (300 pounds × 9 feet) or 2700 foot-pounds of work. If the movers used a 6-foot ramp instead of a 9-foot ramp, a force of 450 pounds would be

To raise a 900-pound piano 3 feet...

...you need a force
of 450 pounds if you
use a 6-foot ramp...

...you need a force
of 300 pounds if you
use a 9-foot ramp...

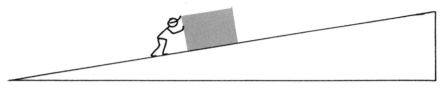

...and you need a force of 150 pounds if you use an 18-foot ramp.

needed to push the piano up the ramp. A force of 450 pounds acting through a distance of 6 feet does 2700 foot-pounds of work, too, because $450 \times 6 = 2700$. If the movers used an 18-foot ramp, then a force of only 150 pounds would be needed to raise the piano into the van, because 150×18 also equals 2700. From all these examples we see that the longer the distance through which the piano is pushed up the ramp, the smaller the force that is needed to do the pushing. If the distance is smaller, then a bigger force is needed to do the same amount of work.

When the movers used a 9-foot ramp, a force of 300 pounds pushing up the ramp had the same effect as a force of 900 pounds pushing straight up. However, a force of 900 pounds is 3 times as big as a force of 300 pounds. So we say that the 9-foot ramp has a *mechanical advantage,* or MA for short, of 3. If the movers use a 6-foot ramp, a force of 450 pounds has the same effect as a force of 900 pounds pushing straight up. Since a force of 900 pounds is 2 times as big as a force of 450 pounds, the 6-foot ramp has an MA of 2. If an 18-foot ramp is used, a force of 150 pounds has the same effect as a force of 900 pounds pushing straight up. Since a force of 900 pounds is 6 times as big as a force of 150 pounds, an 18-foot ramp has an MA of 6.

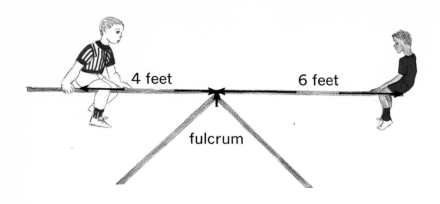

4 feet   6 feet

fulcrum

Levers

A seesaw is an example of the simple machine called the *lever* (LEH-vuhr). Let us see how a light person whose weight pushes down on one side of a seesaw can raise a heavy person on the other side.

Suppose a 60-pound boy is sitting on one side of a 12-foot seesaw. His 40-pound friend wants to ride the seesaw with him. How can the two boys ride the seesaw together? In order for the 60-pound boy to be raised, a force of 60 pounds must push him up. The 40-pound boy can produce a 60-pound force if he sits on the seesaw in just the right place.

The picture on this page shows where the boys must sit on the seesaw so that they can ride it together. Seated like this, when the 40-pound boy moves down through a distance of 3 feet, the 60-pound boy moves up through a distance of 2 feet. The boys just balance each other because a 40-pound force acting through a distance of 3 feet does 120 foot-pounds of work and a 60-pound force acting through a distance of 2 feet also does 120 foot-pounds of work. Since 60 is 1½ times as big as 40, the MA in this case is 1½.

The seesaw in the picture rests on a wooden horse. The wooden horse is its balance point. Every lever has a balance point. The balance point of a lever is called its *fulcrum* (FULL-crum).

A crowbar, the oar of a boat, scissors, tongs and pliers are other examples of levers.

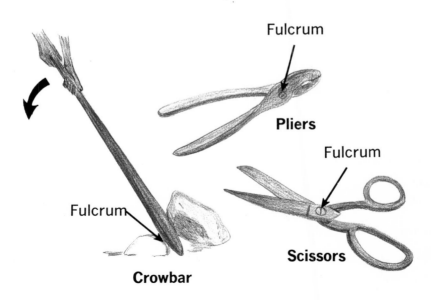

Fulcrum

Pliers

Fulcrum

Fulcrum

Crowbar

Scissors

A capstan

The Wheel and Axle

A *capstan* (KAP-stn) is used for pulling up the anchor of a ship. By pushing on the bars, the sailors make the capstan *rotate*, or turn. As the capstan rotates, the rope to which the anchor is attached winds around the capstan. The sailors walk in a big circle as they push against the bars of the capstan. The rope is wound in small circles around the rotating capstan. A small push by the sailors over the large distance through which they walk is able to lift the heavy anchor inch by inch. The capstan is an example of the simple machine called a *wheel and axle*.

The wheel is a large *cylinder* (SILL-in-der) to which the *axle*, a small cylinder, is attached. The weight to be lifted is attached to a rope that winds around the axle. Another rope winds around the wheel. Because the wheel is larger than the axle, a small downward pull on the wheel rope through a large distance will make a heavy weight attached to the axle rise through a small distance. If the *diameter* (dye-AM-uh-ter) of the wheel is 2 times as big as the diameter of the axle, the wheel and axle has an MA of 2. This means that a force of 100 pounds pulling on the wheel rope can raise a 200-pound weight attached to the axle rope.

The *windlass* (WIND-liss), used for raising a water bucket in a well, is another example of a wheel and axle. The handle, which turns in a large circle, is really the wheel. The barrel to which the bucket is attached is the axle.

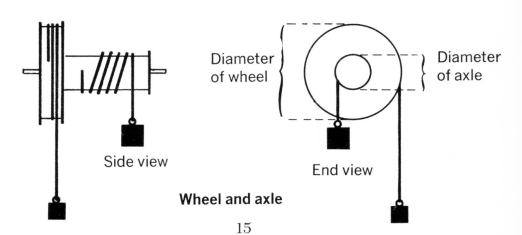

Diameter of wheel

Diameter of axle

Side view

End view

Wheel and axle

15

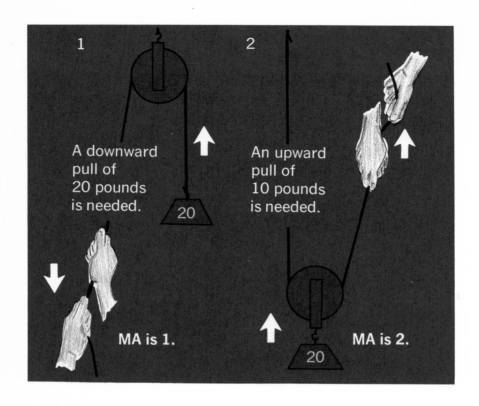

1

A downward
pull of
20 pounds
is needed.

20

MA is 1.

2

An upward
pull of
10 pounds
is needed.

20

MA is 2.

Pulleys

The first picture shows a man using a *pulley* to raise a weight. The man pulls *down* on the free end of the rope. This downward force makes the weight move *up*. The force with which the man pulls down on the rope is the same as the force with which the rope pulls up on the weight. So the MA of this pulley is 1. All that the pulley does, when it is used in this way, is change the direction in which the force acts.

The second picture shows another way of using one pulley. Because two ropes hold up the weight, an upward pull of 10 pounds can raise a weight of 20 pounds. This way of using a pulley does not change the direction of the force. However, this pulley has an MA of 2 because 20 is 2 times as big as 10.

By using many pulleys together, a small force can raise a great weight. Pulleys used together like this are called *compound pulleys*. The great Greek scientist Archimedes (ARK-ih-ME-deez), who lived about 2000 years ago, invented the compound pulley. He once amazed his neighbors by pulling a loaded, three-masted ship up on the beach all by himself. He did this by using compound pulleys.

The drawings show different ways of arranging pulleys so that small forces can lift great weights.

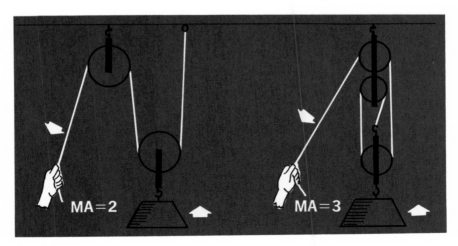

Egyptian slaves pulling a stone block up a ramp

The Inclined Plane and Its Cousin, the Wedge

A ramp is an example of the simple machine called the *inclined plane*. We saw that the same amount of work is done in pushing an object up a ramp as in lifting it straight up. But a ramp makes it possible for a smaller force to do the same amount of work as a force pushing straight up, because the smaller force is acting over a greater distance.

Inclined planes were among the first simple machines used by the early toolmakers. Inclined planes are among the simple machines that all of us use every day of our lives.

The slaves who built the pyramids in Egypt more than 5000 years ago had neither pulleys nor wheels and axles

18

to make their job easier. They were able to place great blocks of stone, weighing as much as one ton, high up in the walls of the pyramids by dragging the blocks up earth ramps.

Mountain roads are built so that they do not go straight up. The force needed to climb a very steep slope is greater than the force automobiles or the legs of most people could produce. So mountain roads slope gradually, winding back and forth with many hairpin turns. Roads built up hills and mountains are inclined planes.

Woodcutters use *wedges* to make the job of splitting wood easier. A wedge is a simple machine made out of two inclined planes placed back to back. The blades of axes, knives, scissors and chisels are all wedges. Nails, pins and needles are also wedges.

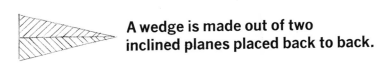

A wedge is made out of two inclined planes placed back to back.

Axe blades and chisels are wedges.

A screw is an inclined plane that is wound in a spiral around a cylinder.

Screws

A *screw* is really an inclined plane that is wound in a spiral around a cylinder, forming grooves and ribs. The ribs are called the *threads* of the screw.

Using a wood screw as an example, let us see how a screw works. As you turn the screw with a screwdriver, the screw moves straight into the wood. So one thing a screw does is change the direction of the force. It changes the direction from turning, or *rotary*, motion to motion in a straight line.

Suppose you give the screw one complete turn. The first picture shows the position of the screw at the start of the turn. The second picture shows the position of the screw at the end of the turn. After a complete turn, the screw has moved the distance between A and B. This distance, the distance between a point on one thread and a point just above it on the next thread, is called the *pitch* of the screw.

If two screws have the same length, the screw with

the larger number of threads has the smaller pitch. It will take more turns to drive this screw into the wood. But it will take a smaller force to drive this screw into the wood. The screw with the smaller pitch has the bigger MA.

A screw that is able to produce a great force is a *jack-screw*. Jackscrews are used for lifting great weights. A jackscrew can even lift a house off its foundation. A jackscrew can produce such a great force because it combines the screw with the simple machine, the wheel and axle. The person operating the jackscrew pushes against a bar that is attached to the jackscrew like the bar of a capstan.

The screw is an important part of many machines. It was used in old fruit presses and printing presses. It is used in vises and clamps. It is used in machines that make tools and in machines that make machines that make tools.

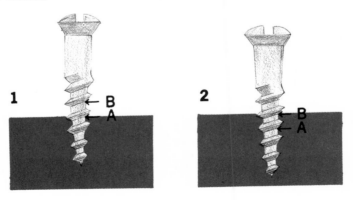

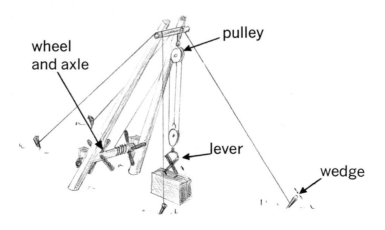

wheel and axle

pulley

lever

wedge

Machines That Are Not So Simple

On page 7 we said that machines, as we usually think of them, are really combinations of simple machines. The crane in the picture was built about 2000 years ago by the Roman engineer Vitruvius (Vih-TROO-vih-us). It combines four simple machines, the pulley, the lever, the wheel and axle, and wedge, into a single machine.

The job of the crane is lifting a heavy weight. The tool for lifting the weight is a pair of tongs attached to a compound pulley. The energy for operating the pulley and tongs is not applied directly to them by the person who operates the crane. The energy is applied to a wheel and axle which *transmits*, or passes on, the energy to the pulley and tongs.

The crane has three main parts. It has a *working part* which does the lifting. It has a source of energy, usually called a *power source.* It has a *transmission,* the wheel and axle, which transmits the energy from the power source to the working part of the crane.

Like the crane in the picture, every machine that is not a simple machine has these three main parts.

Sometimes the working part of a machine may be a single tool. In the case of the spinning wheel, the working part of the machine is the spindle. Sometimes the working part of the machine may be a row of identical tools that all work together. In the case of the modern spinning frame the working part is a row of 100 or more spindles.

A modern spinning frame

The pestle is moved up and down, so the crushing is *not continuous*.

Rotary Motion

Thousands of years ago flour was made by using a *pestle* (PESS-uhl) and *mortar*. The grain was placed in the stone mortar and was crushed by pounding it with the pestle. This way of making flour was not a very good one. While the person using the pestle worked all the time to move the pestle up and down, the pestle crushed the grain only with its downward stroke. The crushing was interrupted whenever the pestle was lifted. So the crushing was not *continuous*.

Flour could be made in a better way by using a *rotary*

quern. The grain was placed between the two millstones. The upper millstone was made to rotate by turning the handle attached to it. The rotating millstone crushed the grain. As long as the millstone turned, the crushing of the grain was not interrupted. Because of the *rotary motion*, the crushing was continuous.

Although man has been making tools for about 500,000 years, he has been making rotating machines for only about 8000 years. The spindle and the potter's wheel are the oldest rotating machines.

Since man made his first rotating machine, he has built the principle of rotary motion into more and more machines. By using the principle of rotary motion, man has built machines that do the same thing over and over again without interruption.

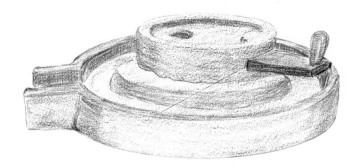

When the handle of the rotary quern is turned, the crushing is *continuous*.

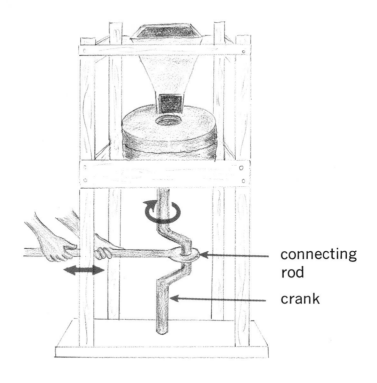

connecting
rod

crank

**The crank and connecting rod change back
and forth motion to rotary motion.**

Transmission

The hand flour mill in the picture on this page was
built about 450 years ago. Like the rotary quern, the
mill has an upper millstone that is free to rotate. The
upper millstone is the working part of the mill. The
power source is the muscle power of the person operating the mill. The transmission of the mill is made up of

a *crank* and *connecting rod*. When the connecting rod is moved back and forth, the crank is made to rotate. The rotating crank makes the millstone rotate. So, while the crank and connecting rod transmit energy from the operator to the millstone, they also change back-and-forth motion to rotary motion. In some machines a crank is used to change rotary motion to back-and-forth motion. The combination of crank and connecting rod is one way of transmitting energy to the working part of a machine.

Energy can also be transmitted to the working part of a machine by means of *wheels and belts*. Another way of transmitting energy is by using toothed wheels called *gears*. While wheels, belts, and gears transmit energy, they can also change the direction of motion. They can be used, too, to increase or reduce the force applied to a machine.

The big gear has twice as many teeth as the little gear. The little gear turns twice as fast as the big gear and in the opposite direction.

Prime Movers

Human muscle power operated the rotary quern and the quern we described on page 26. *Animal power* operated the *donkey-mill* in the picture on this page. A *gasoline engine* provides the power that makes an automobile run. An *electric motor* provides the power that makes a washing machine work. Human muscle power, animal power, the gasoline engine and the electric motor are all examples of *prime movers*. Prime movers provide the power that makes machines run. Prime movers may be living things, like people or animals. Prime movers may be machines, like gasoline engines and electric motors.

Until about 2000 years ago, all machines were operated by either human muscle power or animal power. The crane in the picture was operated by the muscle power of the five men inside the large wheel. The wheel was a *treadmill*. As the men walked, they pushed the wheel back with their feet, making it turn.

With human and animal muscle power as prime movers, the work that machines could do was not very great.

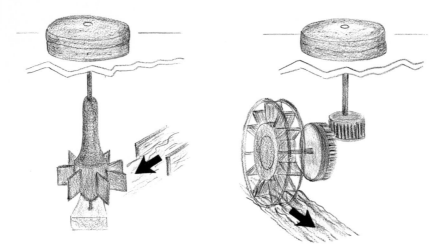

Horizontal water wheel   **Vertical water wheel**
(The arrows show the direction in which the water flows.)

The Waterwheel

The *waterwheel* is a prime mover that is made to work by the force of running water.

The first waterwheels were built about 2000 years ago. They were mounted *horizontally*. The horizontal water-wheel in the picture was used for turning a millstone. The shaft of the waterwheel was attached to the upper millstone. The millstone made a complete turn for every turn of the wheel. So, even though horizontal water-wheels were used only in fast mountain streams, the millstones turned slowly and could grind grain no faster than a donkey-mill could.

30

A better waterwheel was built by Vitruvius, the Roman engineer who built the crane described on page 22. Vitruvius mounted his waterwheel *vertically*. When the waterwheel was mounted in this way, it transmitted power to the machine it operated by means of gears. In the Vitruvian wheel in the picture the gear attached to the millstone had fewer teeth than the gear attached to the waterwheel. As a result, the millstone turned many times every time the waterwheel turned once. So a mill with a vertical wheel could grind grain faster than a mill with a horizontal wheel.

Vertical waterwheels could produce a lot of power. So they were used to operate many kinds of machines. They were used to cut and polish marble. They were used for sawing wood and tanning leather. They were used to operate spinning frames. They were used in iron and papermaking.

The waterwheel had two important disadvantages as a prime mover. Water mills had to be built on or near rivers or streams. This meant that the working machines, operated by waterwheels, had to be placed near rivers or streams. Sometimes rivers and streams ran low. Even when special millponds were built, the water supply might give out. Then the working machines could not operate because of lack of power.

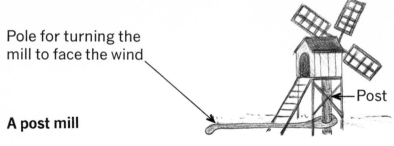

Pole for turning the
mill to face the wind

Post

A post mill

The Windmill

The power of the wind was used for thousands of years to carry ships over the sea. The power of the wind was not used to any great extent as a prime mover until about 800 years ago. The *windmill* is the prime mover powered by the wind. A windmill has sails that are turned by the wind. As the sails turn, they turn gears which turn the working machine.

The earliest windmills were *post-mills*. A post-mill consisted of a little house mounted on a post. The sails were attached to the little house. The gears and working machine were inside. A windmill can work only when its sails face the wind. So the whole mill had to be turned every time the wind changed.

The *tower-mill* was a better kind of windmill. The sails were attached to a tower which was free to turn so that the sails could always face the wind. The working machine was in a building underneath the tower. It was easier to turn the tower and sails than to turn the whole windmill.

Windmills were improved even more when *automatic fantails* were attached to them. The fantails were small sails that worked in such a way that they kept the sails of the windmill facing straight into the wind all the time.

Windmills could produce as much power as water-wheels. They were used to turn millstones and to operate pumps. They were used for sawing wood. In the Netherlands, a flat country where waterwheels could not be used, windmills were used for operating almost every kind of machine.

The windmill has one big disadvantage as a prime mover. Its sails turn only when there is a wind. So when there is no wind, the machines operated by the sails are idle.

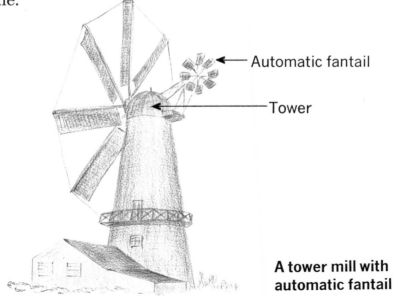

Automatic fantail

Tower

A tower mill with automatic fantail

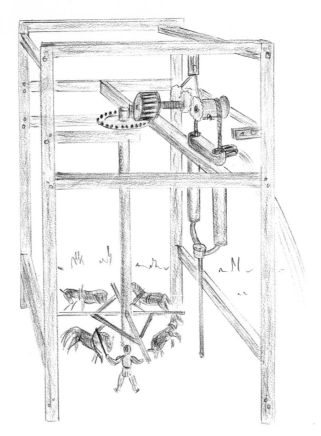

Horses operated this mine pump.

The Steam Engine

People began to use coal a lot as a fuel about 300 years ago because wood was too expensive. As more coal was used, the miners had to dig deeper into the earth for it. Underground water which poured into the mines had to be pumped out. Powerful pumping machines were installed to free the mines of water.

Because coal mines were usually not near streams, waterwheels could not be used to power the pumping machines. Because the pumping machines had to operate even when no wind was blowing, windmills could not be used either. For these reasons, the mineowners used animal power to operate their pumping machines. As deeper mines were dug, more and more animals were needed to operate the pumps. One mineowner had to use 500 horses to keep water out of his mine. This made the mineowners look for other prime movers.

It had been known for a long time that steam could exert a great force. This fact gave engineers the idea that they could use the power of steam as a prime mover.

The first successful steam engine was built by Thomas Newcomen around 1712. Its main parts were a cylinder with a piston inside it that moved up and down, and a boiler. Steam was made inside the boiler when a fire was built underneath it. The steam was piped from the boiler into the cylinder. The weight of the pump rod raised the piston, letting steam into the cylinder. Air pressure pushed the piston down again. The piston was attached to a lever which transmitted the power produced by the engine to the pump.

Although the Newcomen engine was used at many mines, it was very wasteful. It wasted heat because the

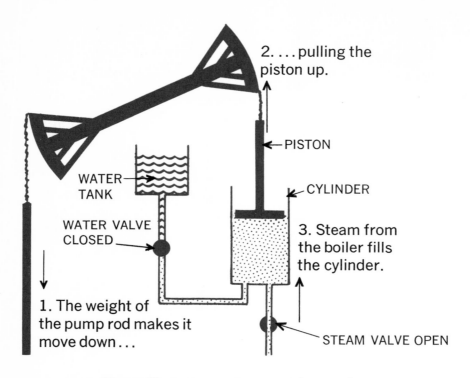

2. . . . pulling the piston up.

PISTON

WATER TANK

CYLINDER

WATER VALVE CLOSED

3. Steam from the boiler fills the cylinder.

1. The weight of the pump rod makes it move down . . .

STEAM VALVE OPEN

How a Newcomen steam engine works

cylinder had to be cooled after the piston moved up so that air pressure could push the piston down again. It wasted heat because the cylinder was not made accurately. As a result, the piston did not fit snugly inside the cylinder. Newcomen's steam engine was wasteful, too, because it produced power only when the piston moved down in the cylinder.

A better steam engine was built about 60 years later by James Watt. Watt found a way of keeping the cylinder

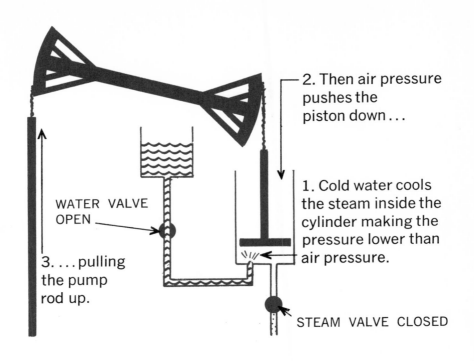

2. Then air pressure pushes the piston down...

1. Cold water cools the steam inside the cylinder making the pressure lower than air pressure.

WATER VALVE OPEN

3. ...pulling the pump rod up.

STEAM VALVE CLOSED

hot all the time. He was able to have his cylinder made accurately so that the piston fit snugly as it moved up and down inside the cylinder. Because of these changes, Watt's steam engine was not as wasteful as Newcomen's engine and needed less coal to make it run. It used only one-third as much coal as other steam engines at the time.

Later Watt built a steam engine that was *double-acting*. It produced power when the piston moved both up and down. Other inventors after Watt improved the steam engine even more by using steam under very high pressure. High-pressure steam engines are very powerful.

Machine Tools

Thomas Newcomen could not have built a better steam engine than the one he made. Nor could James Watt have built his steam engine any earlier than he did. The engines they built were the products of the *machine tools* of their times. Machine tools are power-driven tools for making machine parts. When Newcomen built his steam engine, *boring mills,* the machine tools that bore holes in cylinders, could not bore accurate cylinders that were more than 7 inches across. The cylinder of Newcomen's steam engine had a much larger diameter. Watt was able to make a better steam engine than Newcomen's, partly because a boring mill had just been invented that could bore accurately cylinders that were 50 inches across.

The first accurate machine tools that worked in metal were used by clockmakers and by workshops that made scientific instruments. The screws and other parts that they made, however, were small. Machine tools for making parts of large machines out of metal were not made until much later.

There was no need for machine tools that could make large metal parts because iron was very expensive. So large machines were made of wood, with iron used only at the places that got the most wear. Iron was expensive because of the way it was being made. It was made by heating iron ore, the rock in which iron is found in nature, with charcoal. A lot of wood was needed to make charcoal, however, and wood was scarce.

At the time that Newcomen invented his steam engine, Abraham Darby invented a way of changing coal to coke and using coke, instead of charcoal, in ironmaking. Coal was plentiful, so iron could be made cheaply. When iron became cheap, large machines began to be made of iron. With more large machines being made of iron, accurate machine tools for working large metal parts were needed.

The years between 1725 and 1875 saw the invention of most of the machine tools that are used today. *Lathes, planers, milling machines* and *drilling machines* were some of the machine tools invented during that period. Modern machine tools can work and shape objects of great size with the accuracy of a clockmaker.

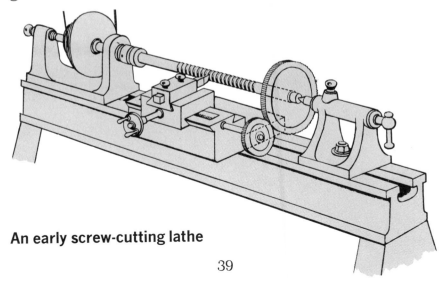

An early screw-cutting lathe

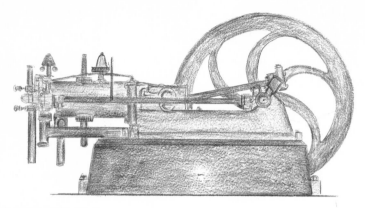

An internal combustion engine built about 100 years ago

New Prime Movers — New Machines

The invention of the steam engine and the cheap price of iron made a revolution in the way people worked and lived.

The steam engine could be moved from place to place. So it was used to power ships and railways. Steamships and steam locomotives made it easier for people to travel great distances. They made it easier for people to move to other places.

Steam engines did not depend on waterpower. So steam-powered mills did not have to hug narrow river valleys. They could be built wherever coal could be carried to them. They could be built where there was space for the towns and cities that grew up around them to spread out.

In the middle of the nineteenth century a new prime mover, called the *internal-combustion engine,* made its appearance. In an internal-combustion engine the fuel is burned right inside the engine. This is different from the steam engine which is really an *external*-combustion engine, because the fuel is burned outside the engine. One kind of internal-combustion engine is the gasoline engine, in which gasoline vapor is burned. Another kind of internal-combustion engine is the diesel engine. The diesel engine uses oil as its fuel.

Internal-combustion engines take up less space and weigh less for the power they produce than steam engines. So gasoline engines are used to power cars, trucks, tractors and airplanes. Diesel engines are used to power some heavy trucks, locomotives and ships.

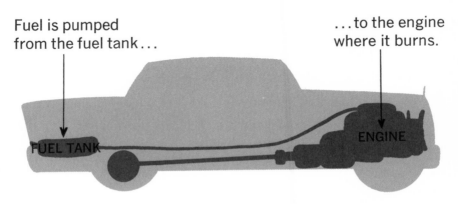

Fuel is pumped from the fuel tank...

...to the engine where it burns.

FUEL TANK

ENGINE

An automobile carries its fuel with it.

Electric power, produced
by generators...

...flows
through wires...

...to homes and factories
where it is used

Electric Power

The steam engine must be near its coal supply. The electric motor, however, doesn't have to be near any fuel supply. The *electric power* needed to run an electric motor is brought to it through wires. So an electric motor can be used almost anywhere.

Most electric power is made by *electric generators* at power stations. The generators may be run by steam power or waterpower. The electric power that is made by the generators then flows through wires to the places where it is used. It may travel hundreds of miles to the prime mover that it runs.

Electric power has made great changes in the way people live. It has made the telephone, the radio and television possible. It has made the lives of people easier by bringing machines into their homes. Refrigerators, vacuum cleaners, air conditioners, dishwashers, and electric shavers are some of these machines powered by electric motors.

Atomic Energy

Most of the prime movers we use today get their power from the energy of burning fuels. The chief fuels we use are coal and oil, or gasoline which is made from oil. It took nature millions of years to make these fuels, but we are using them up very quickly. By the year 2000 there may not be enough coal and oil left to run our engines and generators.

Fortunately, man has discovered another way to obtain energy. This new way is to free some of the energy that is locked inside the atom. *Nuclear reactors* are already being used to free some of the energy that is in the uranium atom. In hydrogen bombs, the energy hidden in hydrogen atoms is released very quickly. Scientists are now looking for a way to release the energy in hydrogen atoms slowly, so that it can be used for doing useful work. When they learn to do this, we will never run out of energy because there is more hydrogen than we can use in the water of the oceans.

Eli Whitney, the inventor of the cotton gin, built the first factory to make machines that had *interchangeable parts*. In 1798 he set up a factory to make muskets for the United States Army. He installed very accurate machine tools in his factory. Then he hired unskilled workers to operate the machine tools. Unskilled workers could operate these machine tools because each tool made only one part. So the job of each worker was easy to learn. All the parts made by one machine tool were exactly alike. After all the parts were made, they were put together or *assembled*. The muskets that were assembled in this way were exactly alike. The parts of one musket could be interchanged with the parts of another, and the musket worked just as well.

Using this system of manufacturing, Whitney was able to make thousands of fine muskets more cheaply than they had ever been made before. This system of manufacturing came to be called the *mass production* system because, using this system, great numbers of identical products could be produced.

Sewing machines, typewriters, bicycles, and automobiles are some of the machines that are made by using interchangeable parts. In a modern automobile factory, conveyor belts speed the parts to the *assembly line,* where the automobile is put together. The first part put on the assembly line is the frame or *chassis* (CHASS-see) of the automobile. As the chassis moves along the assembly-line conveyor, each worker along the line installs a part or tightens a few bolts. When the automobile reaches the end of the assembly line, it is complete. Gasoline is put into its gas tank and it is driven off under its own power.

Because interchangeable parts are used in the manufacture of many machines, it is possible to buy replacements for worn-out parts. So mass-produced machines can usually be repaired easily and cheaply.

Recently another important change has taken place in

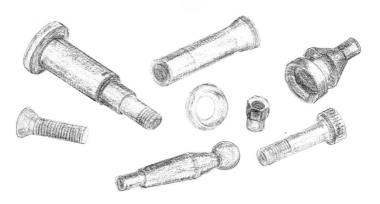

Parts made by an automatic lathe

the way things are made. Many machines are now operated by machines instead of by people. A machine that operates another machine is called an *automatic control.* The automatic fantails described on page 33 and thermostats used for controlling heating systems are examples of automatic controls. With the growth of mass production, more and more machines have been made automatic. Even whole factories have been made automatic, or *automated* (AW-tuh-MATE-ed). When automation has been used, workers have lost their jobs.

Unemployment is a serious problem. The government can help avoid the problems of unemployment. It can help retrain workers who lose their jobs to prepare them for other jobs. It can help make new jobs by getting rid of slums, by building schools and hospitals, and by building recreation centers in which people can spend their free time.

Word List

Automation (AW-tuh-MAY-shun) — The system of operating machines by automatic controls.

Continuous motion — Motion without interruptions.

Crank — A transmission that changes back-and-forth motion to rotary motion or rotary motion to back-and-forth motion.

Fulcrum (FULL-crum) — The balance point of a lever.

Mass production — The system of making products that have interchangeable parts.

Pitch of a screw — The distance between a point on the thread of a screw and the point just above it on the next thread.

Prime mover — A source of power for running a machine.

Rotate — To spin.

Simple machine — A machine which is one of the following: a lever, an inclined plane, a wedge, a pulley, a wheel and axle.

Thread of a screw — One complete turn of the rib that winds around a screw.

Transmission — The part of a machine that passes power from the power source to the working part of the machine.

Treadmill — A moving wheel or platform that is made to turn by animals or men that walk on it.

About the Authors

IRVING and RUTH ADLER have written more than fifty books about science and mathematics. Dr. Adler has been an instructor in mathematics at Columbia University and at Bennington College, and was formerly head of the mathematics department of a New York City high school. Mrs. Adler, who formerly taught mathematics, science and art in schools in the New York area, recently also taught at Bennington. In addition to working with her husband writing this book, she has joined with him on 17 other titles in the *Reason Why* series and drawn the illustrations for most of them as well as for many other books written by him.

Books by Irving Adler alone and books by him in collaboration with Ruth Adler have been printed in 78 different foreign editions, in 11 languages and in 10 reprint editions.

The Adlers now live in the country in Shaftsbury Township, near Bennington, Vermont.

PHOTOGRAPH CREDITS

Page 23 — Bates Manufacturing Co.
Page 45 — Chrysler Corporation